DISPARITY

A COLLECTION OF POEMS

NILANJANA DAS BARMAN

Made with ♥ on the Notion Press Platform
www.notionpress.com

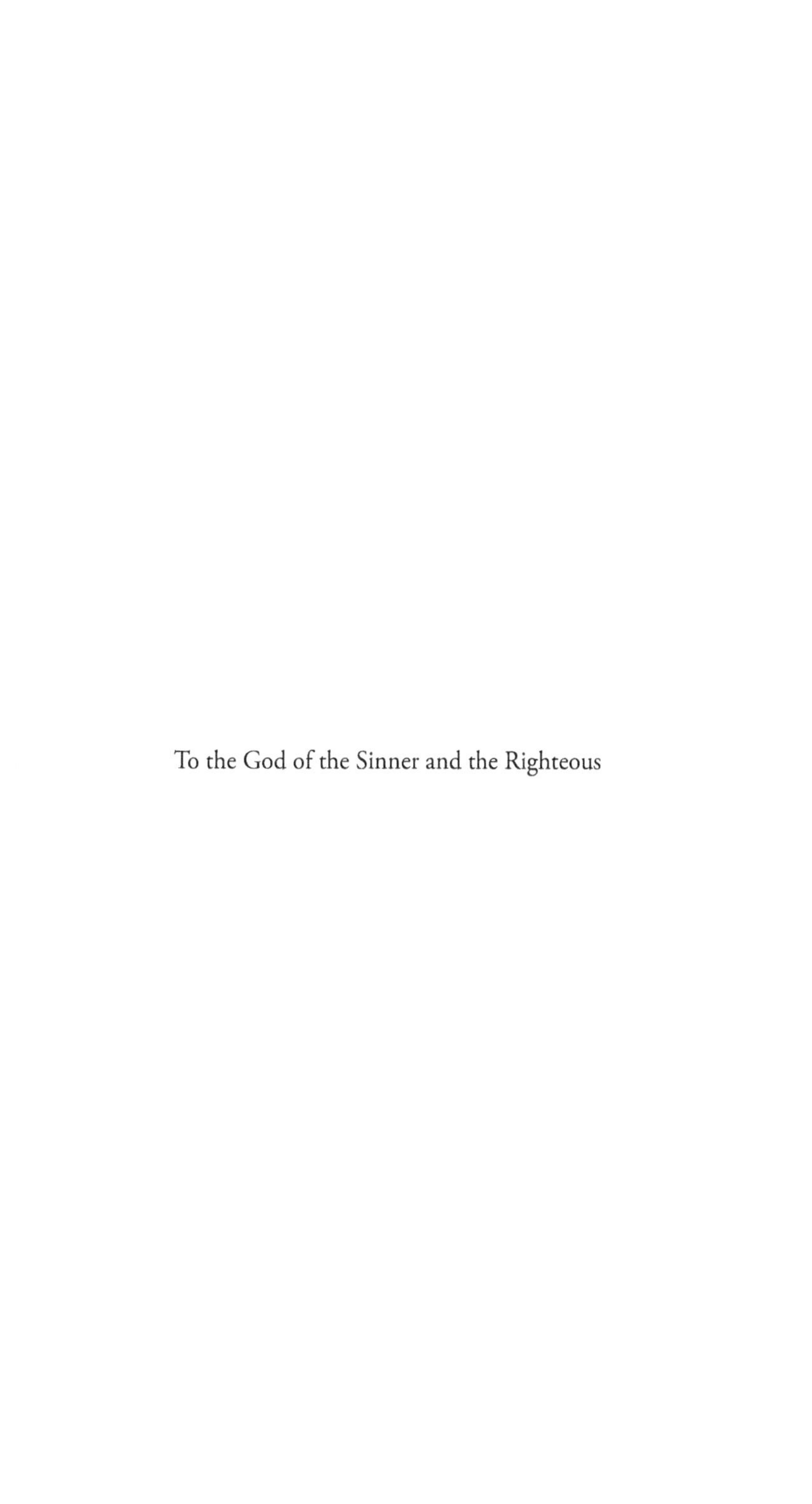

To the God of the Sinner and the Righteous

Contents

Preface

DiSPaRiTy is a collection of twenty poems about the oxymorons of life. Let me clarify. The disparity isn't an oxymoron. It is a contrast of living intermingled with one another. Let us assume a mansion inside a slum or rice fields beside a desert. They aren't supposed to exist but when they do they create something unique. We often use makeup to highlight the features of a dull face. The contrast of highlighter and bronzer creates a sharpness that rivals the edges of a cliff. The disparity in life is what oxymorons are in language. Their existence doesn't dampen the contrast but rather highlights it. Disparities are contradictions living side by side, without confrontation.

We have virtues that we model our lives on. At the same time, there are the vices that make us who we are. These are the grey areas, the half-truths, the compromises, that make life bearable even when they do not necessarily abide by the virtues or vices that we choose to define our identity. There is no such thing as complete joy, absolute pride or utter defeat. Joy comes with the fear of time, pride comes with the threat of shame and defeat comes with the hope of success. They co-exist to make our life what it is.

Dictionary

Definitions from Oxford Languages · Learn more   English ▾

Search for a word   🔍

🔊 oxymoron

/ˌɒksɪˈmɔːrɒn/

noun

noun: **oxymoron**; plural noun: **oxymorons**

> a figure of speech in which apparently contradictory terms appear in conjunction (e.g. *faith* unfaithful kept him falsely true).
> "that fashionable rhetorical novelty, the humblebrag, is itself an oxymoron"

Origin

mid 17th century: from Greek *oxumōron*, neuter (used as a noun) of *oxumōros* 'pointedly foolish', from *oxus* 'sharp' + *mōros* 'foolish'.

The disparity is all around us. Or rather contradictions are all around us. We live in a world full of good and bad. All facts around us are classified as black and white. The reality of life is not limited by these moulds in which we may or may not fit. Life comprises the duality of it all. Love that ends up hurting the lover, Dreams that limit us, Truths that hide, Words that do not express, Hatred disguised as love and vice versa. Life is not black and white. Things are never what they seem, which is exactly what this collection of poems is about.

Acknowledgements

I hereby acknowledge the people who have inspired me to write and inspired my poetry.

I thank my daughter who has been the light of my life from the moment of her birth.

I thank my husband who has been both my support and inspiration to write.

I thank my High School English Teacher, Late Jagadish Chandra Chakroborty, for his encouragement. Even though he is not in the world right now his encouragement continues to be with me.

I thank Jesus for standing by me when no one else did.

And I thank my family for accepting me as I am.

1. Password

There's so much locked behind a password-
My trust in you and yours in me.
The reason behind faked smiles are there,
In confession for selective ears.

Do you read my face when I key in

My eleven letter password?

The only secret I am keen to keep

In waking hours or when I sleep,

The fraction that will forever be mine.

Words pass behind the facade of a password,
Sometimes they hold more sway,
Than the words reverberating in the night air,
Echoing at the depths of a demon's lair.
Reluctantly, yet actively, I hide.

2. Favourite

You ask me my favourite
And I stare at you, wordlessly.
You ask again and I shake my head.
I shake my head.
I have a favourite
But you don't know
My favours lay
highly biased.
In your smile,
In your eyes,
I find the expanse
Of open skies.
You ask me once more,
And I shy away,
My secret safe,
Just for another day.

3. Dear Diary

I don't have much to tell you.
Insignificant details they are.
The colour of the dress I was wearing,
The orientation of the cosmic stars.
Things you can sit and google,
And secrets no one wants to hear,
I don't have much to tell you,
Except for the words that I fear.
The plagues that ravage monuments,
Touch not the shadow of my dreams.
Only my regrets dally and linger,
In the silent nights that scream.
The ink blots when the lines pass through,
Unbidden tears, that you only see.
Scribbled lines and uneven letters
Undulating plains of fragmented truth,
Open to your eyes and hidden from shadows,
The skies shed tears that you withhold.

4. Teddy

Late nights are for cuddling,
So wrap your arms tight.
The winds howl in a frenzy,
Into the cool of the night.
Let your warmth seep in slowly,
As you soak in my tears,
The lightning on the window
Gives form to my shapeless fears.
Desires run havoc,
In dreams that I can't control,
Waking me in a vacuum,
That refuses to unfold.
Late nights are for cuddling,
When stars play hide and seek.
Let your hugs make me stronger,
In moments when I am weak.

5. A Beautiful Mistake

A torn page,

A broken pencil,

A falling house of cards,

A sandcastle invaded by the ravagers of time.

All is not lost,

Though the mistake is beautiful.

Some memories are fossilised

Some hopes remain,

In faded photographs

Of a beautiful mistake.

6. Music

The siren call from aeons past
Floating in the wind.
The tune receding by and by
Ravages my lonely heart.
To the horizon,
Empty and stark,
The silent oak does sing.
With the tune of a phantom Lark
The flute setting high a mark,
The sand slipping past,
The clock hands slowly turn,
Like a spiral long and grand,
The record spins,
On a timeless pin.
Chaos bids adieu
As music flows eternally,
From the cusp of time,
Wave after wave,
Of happenstance,
Witnessing in silence.

7. Unspoken Abuse

"And I love the way you hurt me."
Did I say that out loud?
The accusation in your eyes confirm,
And I lower my head in shame.
I am ashamed of every hurt and pain
Felt at your hand.
I am ashamed that I acknowledge
The reality of that pain.

Love doesn't hurt
But trusts enough to excavate,
Fears and insecurities
All buried deep, somewhat unnaturally.
Insecurities turn to shame
As my pain festers
And my fears aggravate.
Do not cause me for it is too much.
Another hurt stored,
In the vault of unspoken abuse.

8. Lie to me

Lie to me
With the hesitation just there.
Lies are trustworthy
Because of the telling signs I see.
The ever so subtle, blinking of the eye,
The shrugging of shoulders
Tell your truth to me.
Lies are better than half-truths,
Honest omissions that create chasms.
You stand at the other end
Of a rift that widens
With our tectonic plates
Saying faint goodbyes.
Two giants we stand,
Driftwood logs,
Ready to be set aflame,
On barren shores of anonymity.

9. Volcanic Ash

Reports came in like a flood,
About the buried houses
And the emptied streets.
Fumes rising high
From the orifice of creation.
Death followed-
Trailing the bride
Dressed in a pall-
Moving slowly towards
The eternal bridegroom.
Lines blurred between darkness and light
We wait for fire raining down.
We wait,
Till waiting is all we know,
And the steel superstructures wilt,
Like the young sapling in the sunlight,
Wilting and then melting,
Then erasing from pages of history,
As we wait for history to be writting,
In the fire raining down,
In the hope of another rainbow.

10. A Secret Glance

That secret glance
Was supposed to be a secret,
With a lingering hope
And a palpitating heart.
Days turn to months,
Obsessions are made-
Habits and comforts,
All in a glance.
The trees shed leaves,
New flowers bloom,
Fragrant blossoms
House Insects new.
The lingering glance
Looks past the horizon,
Even though gone,
The silhouette remains.
Some silhouettes transform,
Into moving images,
That sometimes talk,
In uncomfortable silences.
Longings last a lifetime,
And obsessions can turn sour,
And secret glances are achieved,

Through keyholes and spywares.

11. Right and Wrong

I am pretty sure you knew the right and wrong of it all,
As you stood aloof on the side,
As you refused to take sides,
Knowing the right and wrong of it all.

> I am not putting you on the stand,
> Nor am I taking the judgment seat,
> I have had time to say my piece
> And I chose to keep the peace.

I know the guilt in your eyes,
Hiding the unsaid lies,
I know the times you hide,
Behind frustrated breathy sighs.

> I am pretty sure that you want to confess,
> Or at least a regret you wish to express
> But I have no use of words you may say
> When you refuse to take a stand for the day.

I have a road with an exit drawn
And a moral compass to guide and warn,
And it leads me far off and away,
So just write to me with all you have to say.

12. Packed and Ready

I am all packed and ready,
The suitcase is full of half-hearted resolutions.
I put in the grey sweater that you wore,
Because it seemed more your colour than mine.
The white lace dress I planned for our wedding
Is tucked right under the shredded jeans.
The little black dress is out at the back,
Along with all the sexy lingerie.

Maupassant is travelling with me,
In a paperback volume, bursting at the seams.
Dickinson keeps me company on cold nights,
When death sounds like a more eager lover.
I packed in the lip balm just in case,
Along with a pack of tampons I may need.
Necessity is a great teacher they say.
I have been taught well to be packed and ready.

The detachment sits ready on my sleeves,
Even when I reach out
With the umpteenth chance.
Change is right around the corner,
Waiting in a taxi with its meter running.
All I have to do is pick up the suitcase,
Cross an imaginary road leading to freedom.

I am packed and ready, have been for a while.
I am just waiting for you to get packed and ready.

13. A Game of Habit

You listen to my lies when I tell you the truth.
I am tired of convincing you of my honesty.
Some assumptions take on flesh,
Through the mundane repetition of habit.

> It's your habit now to see me lie.
> It's my habit now to ignore your jibes.
> It is a game of hide-and-seek
> As you hide behind your half-truths willingly.

You have predetermined truths
That I know you will never confess.
I have untold lies in my mind,
That I will never utter but tell myself.

> A new habit I picked up the other day,
> Staring down your opponent,
> I tried it on your cat who bit me back,
> I liked the confrontation for a change.

We sit in the same room,
Engrossed in our own virtual lives,
Only your one seems almost real,
My one seems and almost lies.

> The tea I made is going cold,
> Just like every day as you feed your cats,
> I play dumb while my hands go numb,

I have no use for this charade of camaraderie.

14. Differences

If I am not better at least I am different,
I am different from the shallow masses,
That paint their faces to hide their scowls.
I don't hide.
Perhaps that doesn't make me a better person,
But I am different enough to try.
I choose to walk the path that leads me home,
Even if the home is not laid with hope.
I walk to my destination binding my destiny.
I walk through all sweat and tear,
Because I have people counting on me.
May be that doesn't make me better,
But I am different from the self-centred crowds,
Who never look beyond their own reflection.
I am different from the faceless masses
Conforming to ideas they don't believe in.
I am my own person swimming against the tides.
I pave my own roads, sometimes leading to disaster.
Yet I forge roads paved in my morality.
Perhaps that doesn't make me better,
But it does make me different,
And these differences always matter.

15. Heaven and Hell

Heaven and Hell-
We wait
With judgemental stares,
Under holy steeples,
Adorn glorified veneers,
Yet the battle rages
In our minds.
Heaven or Hell
Our actions define.

The two wolves raging,
Good and bad,
Look to mate
With our eternal fates.
The one we feed
In our own predilection-
A winner's prize,
A tempting gaze.

Heaven and Hell,
Dwell in our hearts,
Lead us on
To a Bethel of hopes.
Heaven and Hell-
Our crown and chains,

Faith that binds,
Fear that copes.

16. Silent Prayers

Silence amidst the cacophony of confusion,

In the pits of Hades, harboured at the Sea of Soul,

My devotion is ridden with arrows of suspicion-

> I know my bones languish in my misery.

> I am not doing too well, but I don't know better.

> Smiles pain me, laughter is agony,

> Yet the tears provide no relief.

My heart wants to cry out to the God of my salvation,

Yet, my prayers are voiced in silence,

Lest they should cause some offence,

Fear and prejudice guide me.

> My hands reach out to touch

> That distant spectre of comfort,

> Afforded by a divine promise,

> Of the invisible God, through an invisible future.

I am lonely and miserable.

I know I am not doing too well.

It has been a while or perhaps,

It was only yesterday when I last smiled.

> The silence of my God suffocates me-

> My crumbling hope in me,

> In the hope of redeeming myself,

> In the possibility of the resurrection of crumbled dreams

I am in pain and pain is silencing me,

And my bones soak in my loneliness.

I look up for the promise and look down dejected.

I bow down in submission and look up for the promise again.

17. Loving Another

Being you is perhaps the most challenging job-
Looking past wrinkles to decipher the smile,
Distinguishing laughter, crying, sighing, and a sob
A cauldron of emotions abrupt yet sublime.
How do you look into my eyes that doubt my loyalty to you,
And place your claim on my body mind and soul?
How do you pry open the cast iron casket,
And thus, excavate a heart forged in gold?
I envy your optimism and salute your smile.
I bow down to the power you exert on my mind.
My body hums in the assurance of your bliss,
All that promise from an age-old kiss.
Anticipation tied in a cotton thread of longing,
Master and lover, reason and belonging.
Tie me in a cocoon of familiarity that endures.
I may want to run but my heart is yours.

18. Forgiving

Whenever I heard the phrase
Horns of a dilemma
I imagined a two-horn rhino.

The dilemma never faced me,
Till I chose to forgive you,
Thinking that it would show my superiority.

But now I am a mess,
Regretting letting go,
Of the scapegoat, I blame for every single tear shed.

I am in a quandary,
Whether to let my old love for you skin me alive,
Or the newfound love of my saviour,
Lead you to my satisfaction.

The dilemma remains,
And though forgive I must,
Do I forgive the man
Or do I forgive the misgivings?

19. They Came Calling

Death came knocking at the brink of life,
And I faced both with equanimity.
I had a lot to say to both,
But I took their glares in stride.
I had a lot to live for and die,
I chose to do both, but in time.

> Life sauntered by at the point of death,
> And I welcomed her with open arms.
> Death would take offence,
> But I did not say goodbye,
> I could not say goodbye,
> For we had to meet again.

20. Healing

Pieces of me,
Wrapped in gauge,
Stained crimson from wounds,
That persists to heal not.
Touches of love,
Do not reach,
Through the depth,
Of protective indifferencc.

We are broken, all in our own ways.
All come with broken hearts,
Some with broken smiles, others with broken spines.
Reality breaks us little by little
Till we learn to live with all the jangling pieces
Ringing against our ears
Desensitised to hear cries of help.

We break each other,
By our blindness,
By the blindfolds wrapped tightly around unfeeling eyes
Complementing unfeeling hearts,
Empowered by insensitive words.

The pieces are all there-
Inside me, inside you,
All broken but hanging on,

By frayed threads.

There's always a tomorrow for healing
But the healing never comes
While it's still today.
The clock turns,
Time fades,
And tomorrow turns to yesterday.

...

We are all still waiting to heal.

About The Author

Nilanjana Das Barman is a Physics teacher by qualification and a poet and author by passion. She has published several volumes of poetry, novels, and Christian devotionals, and has participated in more than eighty anthologies, some under the pseudonym of Anavah Moses.

She also has four published papers in international journals under her maiden name of Nilanjana Bhadra.

Under the pen name, her poem has found its place in the BIPOC issue 2021 of the Wingless Dreamer.

You can check out her website at www.nilanjanadb.wordpress.com.